Milk a

Milk and Honey
A Celebration of Jewish Lesbian Poetry

Edited by Julie R. Enszer

BODY LANGUAGE 07

A MIDSUMMER NIGHT'S PRESS

New York

For Kim, not a Jew, the one I choose.

Cover photograph © Massimo Caregnato
www.flickr.com/photos/massimocare/

A Midsummer Night's Press
16 West 36th Street
2nd Floor
New York, NY 10018
amidsummernightspress@gmail.com
www.amidsummernightspress.com

Grateful acknowledgement is given to the editors of the following publications in which many of
these poems first appeared (sometimes in a different form): "13 Ways of Looking at 9/11" © 2009
Lesléa Newman. First published in Nobody's Mother, published by Orchard House Press.
Reprinted by permission of Curtis Brown, Ltd. "If Everything that Burns" © 2004 Sima Rabinowitz.
First published in The Jewish Fake Book (Elixir Press, 2004). Reprinted by permission of the
author. "For Despina" © 2010 by Marilyn Hacker. Reprinted from Names: Poems by Marilyn Hacker
by permission of W. W. Norton & Company, Inc. "From Mother Tongue" © Maya Kuperman.
Previously published in the book Mother Tongue (Hakibbutz Hameuchad Publishing House Ltd.,
Tel Aviv, Printed in Israel 2007). Reprinted by permission of the author. "From The
Mountain Mother is Gone" © Sharron Hass. Previously published in 'Em ha-har ne'elma (Helicon
Tag, 1997). Reprinted by permission of the author. and translator "The Lies that Save Us" © Lisa
Dordal. First published in Bridges: A Jewish Feminist Journal, V. 12, N. 2, 2007. Reprinted by
permission of the author. "The New Egypt" © Robin Becker. Previously published in Domain of
Perfect Affection (University of Pittsburgh Press, 2006). Reprinted by permission of the author.

Acknowledgements
I am grateful to all of the writers who submitted work for this collection; their work
demonstrates that the dream of a common language is now a reality. I am
enormously grateful to and appreciative of Lawrence Schimel. The opportunity to
work on this project was a dream, and Lawrence is a true champion and collaborator.

Designed by Aresográfico www.diegoareso.com

First edition, September 2011.

ISBN-13: 978-0-9794208-8-7
ISBN-10: 0-9794208-8-1

Printed in Spain.

Contents

•••

•••

II. HONEY

Introduction

Milk & Honey. What G-d promised Moses would flow from the land, the good and spacious land, where Jews would reside after leaving Egypt. *Milk & Honey.* The literal and metaphoric fluids of women. The sweet and the silky that flows from our bodies and infuses our poetry. *Milk & Honey.* A new anthology of poetry by Jewish lesbians.

The land flowing with milk and honey is an imagined place of plenitude; it is not a geographic location, not an actual state fraught with political complexity; it is a space for our imagination. The land flowing with milk and honey is an ample space with room for our full selves—lesbian, queer, Jewish, political, religious, spiritual, secular. Yet, even in our imagined land of milk and honey, there is conflict, disagreement, the splitting of hairs. In our imagined place of plenitude, there are active negotiations among disparate beliefs, ideologies, and values. In the imagined land of milk and honey, we celebrate, articulate, and elaborate our identities, our commitments, and our lives. We reflect and negotiate the internal and the external. It is political work. It is spiritual work. It is poetic work.

While editing *Milk & Honey,* I reread two earlier Jewish lesbian anthologies, *Nice Jewish Girls* (Persephone Press, 1982) and *The Tribe of Dina* (Beacon Press, 1989). *Milk & Honey* is inspired by these earlier works, and, I hope, it honors them. *Nice Jewish Girls* and *The Tribe of Dina* crystalized an intersectional identity of Jewish and lesbian. *Milk & Honey* elaborates this identity, exploring it in the contemporary world, explaining it for a new generation, and troubling it—playing with not only lesbian but also queer. Poems in *Milk & Honey,* some by poets in the earlier anthologies and many by new poets, extend and continue the conversations of what it means to be Jewish and lesbian, what it means to be Jewish and queer.

The poems of *Milk & Honey* are organized into two parts. The two sections of the book are in a dialogue with one another; just as within each section, the poems are in conversation. The poems of *Milk & Honey* address an array of issues about Jewish lesbian experience – relationships between and among women, family relationships, politics, solitude, ethical responsibilities, history, solidarity, and community. Some poems are serene; they delight readers through close observation. Other poems are noisy and unruly. There is as much cacophony within the collection as there is sonority. Would we want to have our conversation any other way? The poems of *Milk & Honey* ask questions: what does it mean to be Jewish and lesbian today?, how shall we live our lives?, to whom do we bind our future? Even as they reach for answers, the poems raise more questions. Listen. Listen to the words, these poems, as they flow from an imagined land of *Milk & Honey*.

Julie R. Enszer

FEBRUARY 2011

I. Milk

ELLEN ORLEANS

Minyan

"You count now," the preacher said, "You didn't even count before."
from *"The River,"* Flannery O'Connor

Thirteen is magic. When you reach it,
Bar Mitzvah, you will count as a man.
Or, if you are a girl, as a woman.

But not really.

To touch the Torah, our holy of holies,
you will not count. To wear tefillin and tallis,
you will not count. In the Minyan, you will not count
even though that is where you want to
count most, among the worshippers.

Inclusion necessitates exclusion.
Maybe you're in the wrong place.

You leave. Find your own unreliable place.
You learn to count words, frogs, square feet.

You decide
you will decide
what counts.
Birds. Faith. Friends.

You no longer count the minutes.
They have their own unearthly speed.

You count and you don't and you do,
yet you still want to be counted,
this need so inlaid.

When the call comes, *Chevra Kaddisha*,
asking you to sit with the
94-year-old body, even though
you've left, you also have not.
You say yes.

You, dead of night. You,
in the mortuary.

You, a *minyan*
of one.

ELLEN BASS

Loving A Woman

I was nineteen and on LSD
the only time God spoke to me.
Or, if not God, a voice so clear
and clearly not my own
it could have been the creek,
still so clean we could bow
and drink. The day was warm,
a thrum of insects, budding of cells,
the fat leaves opening their pores,
the building up of sugars
and the breaking down,
the tree's green breath
spilled into my lungs.
I sat in the stream, a stone
the water washed over,
wearing away each roughened surface.
On the other shore, she
lounged against a boulder,
branches above her,
framed in a darkling shrine.
The voice could have been
the air itself, saying:
Nothing you could do
would ever be wrong.

The words entered me like the sun
pouring into the mouths
of chlorophyll, as the leaves stirred,
as the light sifted down
on her slight shoulders,
her freckled cheekbones.

ROSE FOX

Unticheled

When I am being a boy
I put on a suit with well-shined shoes.
My partner says,
"You look ready for your bar mitzvah."

Friends suggest accessories:
Hipster glasses. A heavy watch.
My ex-girlfriend says,
"You need a yarmulke."

I'm as Jewish as I am a girl: born to it but half-hearted.
I never studied Hebrew or the Torah.
All I know how to say
is "Mazel tov" and "Baruch dayan ha'emet."

But maybe someday I will wear a kippah
with my suit and well-shined shoes.
Then I can say,
"Today, I am a man."

SIMA RABINOWITZ

If Everything That Burns

If everything that burns   (fire)
        or slackens to rest   (Sabbath)
everything that is light alone   (honey)
        or none at all   (sleep)
is a sixtieth part of something else
where are you, beloved, in this equation
        the bright wilderness   (dream)
where what cannot be counted
        wanders between this world and the next   (prophecy)

        I make my home in Paradise
                        with you.
        Your rounded thighs like jewels:
                        silver, saffron, rose, and cedar.
        Your eyes:
        the only sea.

Promise me, woman who rises from the desert,
you will remember the days of our desire   in the world to come.

BONNIE MORRIS

Ruth: separated from Naomi

Me
Left me
You left me
Before you left me
Me before you left me
Kissed me before you left me
Had kissed me before you left me
You had kissed me before you left me
Only you had kissed me before you left me
If only you had kissed me before you left me
If only you had kissed me before you left
If only you had kissed me before you
If only you had kissed me before
If only you had kissed me
If only you had kissed
If only you had
If only you
If only
If

JENNY FACTOR

A Noah Story

After the 40th day and the 40th night,
my breath caught in the sinew of my body.

Everything heaved together. The waters
receded, and then the dark. With a

clack and a scuffle, a broken branch
dragged across the window. A winded dove

found the avocado tree in our yard, and found
it good, frittered with a frightened voicebox

from lawn to table. To wire. To tree again.
A skunk scampered down our driveway

with five babies keeping pace under her tail.

And I was here, finally and at last, in my
40th year, in the middle of my life

Awake in my body.

LISA DORDAL

The Lies that Save Us

Driving through Georgia,
we lie like Abraham.
Are you sisters?, people ask.
Yes, we answer. Twins, even.
Though we are dressed similarly
in broad-brimmed hats,
long-sleeved shirts and tan pants
tucked into thick, white socks
(it being tick season and all) –
we look nothing alike.
Thought so, people say,
as if they have figured out
some secret code. We smile back,
knowing the power of things unseen:
of atoms, quarks, and auras
and all the love that lies between.
Kissing energy, we call it.
But all they can see is
something.

BONNILEE KAUFMAN

Middle Aged

All my life the work ethic
For what, twelve hundred dollars
A month, I live.
I go through money
The way dandruff
Rains down on shoulders
Of a black shirt worn
With oblivion.

Think I was born stuck
Inside out
Upside down
Strangled, so *nu?*
They had to tug and
Pull genetic burdens
Heavy as wet woolen blankets
My backbone is stooped.

Middle aged,
Should be wearing purple
Years ago,
I flashed this badge of lesbian,
Appropriated now
By everyone else, blenderized.

I wonder
Where all the renegades are?

Should have wisdom spewing
Wrinkles, wisdom worthy of these
Drooping knees no longer fashionable
Instead, I keep waiting
To grow up, stop disassociating
Crumbling into chopped liver.

Coming from a long line
Of sour wheeler-dealers
Cars repossessed in the
Night, nothing to run after
But a bad deal
Bloody and track marked
"Bail me out" my role model
This father of mine
He begged.

Other cultures require pulling
Hair out of grief I have
Bald spots, patches
Held in my hand
Grieving bad deals
Never learning from
Mistakes or geography
I cannot begin to explain the
Continental divide, always at

The low end of the
Learning curve my
Worth flat lines
There is no why
I give up, take too little.

After the coals burn down
Embers form like promises:
Meditative mind, pure calm.
I submit, who wouldn't?
Willing to give it all, again
Forgetting the meaningless
Value of a kiss, Judas
Stands before me
Stringing quack jewels
Round and round my
Neck, lining his pockets.

JOANNA HOFFMAN

Sh'ma

> *Sh'ma Yisrael, Adonai elohenu, Adonai ehad*
> *Hear Israel, the Lord our God, the Lord is one.*

The Sh'ma was always my favorite prayer
because it was short and to the point
unlike those other prayers that droned on and on
in an ancient language I only understood in fragments.
On Yom Kippur, the Day of Atonement
I would sit in the synagogue and think about food
or girls I had crushes on with Biblical names
praying to my own gods—
the goddess tori amos, the god of chicken soft tacos, the god of
      sexual confusion
because the wrathful Jewish god Yahweh we were taught to cower
      under
seemed like a jerk
seemed a lot like my own father
who walked around all day with a scowl
burning like a bush inside his angry heart.

The rabbi's told us we had better ask forgiveness
better pray hard enough, long enough, strong enough.
It reminded me of how my mother would say,
"wait till your father gets home"
and I would cower under the bed

and bite tiny prayers onto my fingers.

The image of him, red-faced and furious
burned into my mind
arising like smoke every time I scratched the car, failed a math
        test, stayed out past curfew.

It's hard to love an angry God, one whose smiles rumble like
        thunder
setting off car alarm warnings, wailing, splitting canyons down
        tear ducts.

Last year I stood next to my father at the airport
and suddenly I realized we had the same stance
arms folded, left foot out.
When I told him, he smiled and told me 'I know'.
And I gradually began to see
the parallels between us
—our ridiculous stubbornness, the flecks of soft brown in our eyes
the way our hearts break, egg shells crackling around rusted iron cores
the way we forgive each other, wax softening down to solid pools
        of marble

Namaste
means the god in me
greets the god in you.

I don't think my father would understand
but when i hear that word

my heart unfurls
and i see in him, in me, in all of us
so much possibility.

So I tell my dad, "Don't worry about me."
I tell that nun, "Don't pray for me."
I'm gonna be just fine.
My god thinks I'm awesome.
Scrawls 'I love you' onto birthday cards.
Breaths 'I'm proud of you' into my ear
every time I get up to read poetry
Whispers 'it's okay,'
every time some bitch twists knives into my heart.
Loves me the way
I wanna love my kids
Like everything they touch turns to heaven;
Like the power of god resonates from their smiles;
Like the sound of their laughter
is the only prayer
they will ever need.

JOAN ANNSFIRE

Ohio Ice Storm

We lived in a blizzard of ignorance
in the fifties, on Cleveland's East Side,
the neighborhoods blanketed by covenants,
we lived only where permitted,
surrounded by an antagonism
merciless as the wind coming down from the lake;
deep and suffocating
as new snow.

The kink in a follicle of hair,
the bony protrusion of a nose,
the syllables of a name,
these were the dangers that spelled trouble,
a need to be circumspect,
to deflect attention.

Friends from other backgrounds
assured me I was not like the others,
wealthy, mercenary or snobbish
and I held their special dispensation
as the highest form of praise.

We were only a few years beyond
the stories, the film footage;

Europe buried under
massive mountains of gold teeth,
eyeglasses, human hair.

Huddled together, we listened
to the McCarthy hearings,
remembered the Rosenbergs,
speculated as to how far things might go
in this unpredictable, new land
where hatred churned
beneath a placid, frozen surface,
smooth and hard
as Lake Erie ice.

MELANIE KAYE-KANTROWITZ

Grogging

if i could stop here. if it hadn't happened. it's purim, ramadan. last
night erev purim a continent apart we each went to queer shul to
hear how a jewish woman saved her people from massacre. at cbst
sharon the rabbi wore shorts, the crowd was raucous, many in
costume, in drag. in the row behind me three women all in black
leotards with pink netting around the waist, and a pink net puff in
the hair, waved pink puff wands. they sat with their children and i
couldn't tell which child was whose. when it came to the part where
the king orders vashti to dance naked, and she refuses absolutely,
read the text, we all clapped and hurrahed and one of the pink-net
women shouted absolutely, absolutely, vashti refuses absolutely and
shook her wand. i loved her fierceness. and when vashti is exiled –
when esther replaces her– a scab– i wanted you there with me

then came a break for the children's costume contest, the winners,
like the non-winners, adorable: a tiny girl cow – the announcer
called her by name, our chana the cow. the second winner was a
boy knight, he came from the row of pink-net women and when
his victory was announced (and he, like the cow, won a fine
wooden grogger) the whole row of pink net women and children
cheered wildly and shouted, rafi, rafi. they weren't afraid to be so
out there cheering for their boy. he beamed and flashed his tinfoil
sword, not afraid to be caught feeling pride and pleasure, and i
thought, that child is loved.

then i went to the bima to read the part where esther denounces haman to the king, i got to say, IT IS HAMAN! and everyone grogged and grogged and i sat down, while the story takes haman to the high gallows, the grogging a bit muted, some of us troubled by bloodlust.

last night a continent apart we heard in shul how a jewish woman saved her people from massacre. this morning the news. hebron. the tomb of abraham. their foreheads were touching the floor, in prayer. the blood.

today a continent apart four o clock finds us each at the israeli consulate to say with our bodies, A JEW DID THIS NOT IN OUR NAME. Baruch Goldstein a doctor. one funeral home refused to prepare his body. in his eulogy the rabbi said, one million arabs are not worth one jewish fingernail. i want to carve the words out of his heart, his jewish heart i would give anything to disown. the chosen chosen chosen. if sarah and hagar had cheered for each other's children. we are all worth exactly the same, priceless

JENNIFER MARGULIES

Need

I was a glutton for it by any name,
although I think I lost at least ten pounds
in those ten months with you. I wanted only
you for sustenance. Punchdrunk, moonstruck,
I never left my place, not even when
what once had nourished me was gone. It was
not hope but only animal instinct.
In Yiddish, people *ess;* animals *fress.*
Ess und fress: one word for those who think,
another for the ones that only feel.
Insatiable as any squint-eyed infant,
a baby sucking air, sucking a finger,
I felt no heart behind your breast and still
closed my lips around the hunger and held on.

ELEANOR LERMAN

Sunday Brunch in Orange County, California

Huevos rancheros and mimosas at the
hardwood bar, just to set the scene
All the colors migrate, liquefy as we
get drunker. The football highlights turn
into angelfish that kiss us and swim away

Then there are the women's arms
wrapped in sliding silver—real silver,
silvery to look at, like manacles of money
And what did we talk about to pass the time?
The Christmas parade of yachts
and shopping trips to the Inland Empire
in a blue car. A beautiful car that
ate the miles like a magical bird might
eat the sky. A blue sky. Luscious. Alive

Me? I don't regret a moment of it—me,
who pretends never to even mention myself
Easier to hide behind some fanged revenant
slouching down the highway
Easier to pretend that nothing has been easy,
that there is no spa music playing
in my headphones. *Buddha's Dream,*

Healing Melodies: who said I didn't know
how to access the channel that tunes them in?

Easier to pretend that I never even mention myself
But it's true: here in my dark haven of dread
I admit that I am not happy anymore and I remember
what I want. Or will want, in the hour of the deluge
How much, after all—and in the end—can
one human being be expected to connect with others?
The manacles of love, the manacles of money
You wake up and they are broken
You wake up and no one speaks to you but God

Oh yes, Him. The sly Hebrew who is where
He is when He wants to be, except when
He is not. Today, he wants a drink, He wants
a woman. He wants to love us all and then vanish
into the long blue sky. Reconciling His absence
is all I have been thinking about. I invite you
to join me. Your guess is as good as mine

ROBIN BECKER

The New Egypt

I think of my father who believes
a Jew can outwit fate by owning land.
Slave to property now, I mow
and mow, my destiny the new Egypt.
From his father, the tailor, he learned not
to rent but to own; to borrow to buy.
To conform, I disguise myself and drag
the mower into the drive, where I ponder
the silky oil, the plastic casing, the choke.
From my father, I learned the dignity
of exile and the fire of acquisition,
not to live in places lightly, but to plant
the self like an orange tree in the desert
and irrigate, irrigate, irrigate.

SHARRON HASS *Translation by Amalia Ziv*

From The Mountain Mother Is Gone

6

Far from the guests' mind scattered
in the garden like half-bitten raisins,
Inanna, queen of heaven and earth,
leans against the *huluppu* tree, and laughingly greets
the magnificent slit opening between her legs

Her body is a just beginning
wonder

26

Even in ignorance we knew
that the fields are sacred. A place of
undisturbed growth. At their border we left
the iron hooves and embarked on the green road
the road to the body infused with sky and danger.
At the body's axis swayed a tree
and in the hair's darkness blossomed nests of stars
but desire already was
a missing Cyclops' eye, mocking

Drawing near to the body
as to the end of the birds' journey

certainty is historical: genetic.
The certainty of distances.

We did not know the body was but a threshold,
a rock stopping a far and diving deep
from which no echo returns

58 Close-Up
I have to write of you, like a child
that must give names to the darkness —
to stop my shattering into loneliness
my face composing what is hanging in the air.
I have to say many azure words
to free you from the stone
in which we are confined.
Even if the clouds are voiceless
their weight draws me down to the grass, to the goldfish
that grew pale in the sun,
close to the face of an ant I see
her, like us, caught up in a sort of feistiness
gathering from hand
to mouth.
And the body is all caverns, deep sand castles
that rose up, once, like a storm from the void, when you came

ELANA DYKEWOMON

An Eastern/Western Country Song

for my mother with whom I can discuss almost anything

We don't talk about zionism any more
because I say
we're on the wrong side of a brutal war
and you say
the Arabs would push us from the shore
into deep water
and I say, mother
it's the Israelis who are shoving
I say why not count
the peaceful
the nonviolent protests
and you say
they're deceiving you
and I say
let's not talk about zionism any more
we're on the wrong side of a brutal war
and you say
you had to get the last word in
and I say ma
I saw the separation wall in Bilin
the farmers soldiers were teargasing

I say we can't leave this
to politicians
and you say
I don't know my history
it's no mystery
let's not talk about zionism anymore.

LESLEA NEWMAN

13 Ways of Looking at 9/11

I.

First thought:
This is not good
for the Jews.
Second thought:
This is not good
for the lesbians.
Third thought:
this is not good
for me.

II.

Even now—especially now
the body has its demands:
the belly cries to be fed.
But food can't push past
the lump of tears
stuck in my throat
too terrified
to spill from my eyes

III.

The cats, usually so aloof
except at feeding time

stay close
unaware, yet knowing
something heavy
soft and purring
is needed on my lap

IV.

Born in Brooklyn
raised on Long Island,
I moved to the East Village
to make my fortune
then fled the city
twenty years ago.
Still, in my heart
I am a New Yorker
so people call,
wanting to connect
wanting it to be their tragedy, too.
"Did you lose anyone?"
they ask, almost hopeful.
I am almost sorry to disappoint them.

V.

The nation is on high alert.
I stock canned goods in the basement,
stash two hundred dollars
under my mattress
thinking, *this and a token*
will get me a ride on the subway.

Then I remember
where I live
there is no subway

VI.
The search dogs get depressed;
there are so few bodies to be found.
One team stages a mock recovery
to boost their dogs' morale.
A burly firefighter
puts down his gear,
lies down in the rubble
and like a dog, plays dead.
Soon the search dogs start to bark
and wag their tails
and lick his face.
Soon the firefighter rises from the ashes
and slowly walks away

VII.
Bags and bags of body parts:
finger, ankle, elbow.
I remember lying in bed with you
looking at our feet sticking up
from under the blankets,
yours so brown and slender,
a perfect size six with ballerina arches;
mine so pale and squat and flat.
We joked about knowing each other in a crowd

solely by our feet.
Now I try to wrap my mind
around the unimaginable:
a knock at the door,
a strange man
brings me your right foot
and I am grateful even for that.

VIII.

It doesn't take long
for the newspapers
to quote letters
blaming Israel and the Jews.
It doesn't take long
for the newspapers
to quote Jerry Falwell
blaming the feminists and the gays.
It doesn't take long
for me to stop reading
the newspapers.

IX.

In my little town
at my little grocery store
a cashier refuses to check out
a woman he calls a "turban head,"
a woman I call a cancer survivor.

X.

It is the longest we have gone
in thirteen years
without making love.
Finally I let you touch me
though I feel I might shatter
like glass. Those who died
will never enjoy
this gift again.
How dare I waste it?

XI.

A blank notebook page
an empty computer screen,
What is the point of writing anything?
Then an unbidden email from a fan:
"Thank you for bringing so much
beauty into my heart and the world."
Tears tumble from my eyes.

XII.

I dream a child stands
on the twin towers
of her sturdy legs.
before she disappears
and I am running
across the Brooklyn Bridge,
naked and burning,
my skin falling away

like the Vietnamese girl
in that famous photo.
Everyone I ask for help
asks me, "Are you an Arab
or a Jew?" I tell them,
"I am a human being"
and everyone who hears my answer
vanishes like smoke

XIII.

On Rosh Hashannah
There is a discussion group at the synagogue.
Our leader says when she first heard,
she was so angry she wanted to kill
somebody—anybody—and everybody
she spoke with felt the same way.
"Is there anyone here
who isn't furious?" she asks.
I look around the circle,
then slowly raise my hand
like a white flag of surrender.

II. Honey

JOAN NESTLE

Words to the Woman in the Hat, Rosa Luxemburg

Melbourne, 2010

Rosa, 10 steps and you reach the wall,
Orchids blossom in the strength of your desire
To see beyond the final No
Of a State enamored with a war.
Perfumes overcome exclusions,
Hints of life become huge things,
The flutter of a wing, the bellows of a bull,
Sunlight given to you only on the slant
Kisses your body into being.
I come to you, Jewish woman to Jewish woman,
Hair and hip, mouths in love with thought,
To touch your body with my own
Before the rifle thrust that ends your dreaming
Of the end of nations.
I come from a land of walls.
Come, mount me,
We have skies of work to do.
How Jewish are we, how queer are we?
My breasts and belly, my thighs and mouth, my open hand wide
        against your pleasure
Will take on histories, will buck against the soldiers at the borders.

Not milk and honey, that would be a phony sweetness in such
　　　　times as these
Not milk and honey, Rosa, this you knew—rather, a fierce want
　　　　that breaks the normal, the national,
How Jewish are we? How queer are we? Enough to refuse.

Breath

We never go to bars, lover, we stroll right past
the bright, damaged signs designed
to polish and replenish

the damaged brightness
of the hammered city canyons
in which you've grown and outgrown

version after version of desire.
We stroll past trees and singing strangers,
sometimes holding hands, sometimes sliding

finger against finger, sometimes strolling side by side
alone through loneliness, separate renditions
of pulpy disappointed houses

haunting the fringes of our happiness
in strolling past them. Sometimes
we're brand-new animals holding brand-new hands

and sometimes we're sculpted, cut and shaped and labeled
by the eyes of strangers
who notice I feel sexier with you

than with the cutest, cleverest, best-built man –
wait, is he gay too? –
and sometimes the future we're beginning to remember

circles our shoulders, guiding us back
to the moment of Creation
curling in our bed, naked and nervous,

a wisp of time and space
frozen into a sexual breath, the breath
in which God says

"Let there be" or "It is good,"
the breath I take
when I feel your fingers

scouting my uncreated places, small white keys
unlocking the strangeness
of our differences, our little worries and toughened hearts

softening like raspberries
under the hot but hidden sun of love
that promises and shadows so much, glittering

on the Caribbean I become
as you unhalter my skin, whispering something
neither of us will remember

a moment later
when God has taken
our still-untaken breath.

JESS NOVAK

Mischling

I wish I could tell you
about some sisterhood that arose between
us, some twinning of pomegranates.
She couldn't get the temperature right
in the shower, and kept turning around, shifting
her scant weight from one foot to the other.
Her shirt slung over a shoulder,
she was wearing this perfect black skirt that hung
on her ass, and I wanted it, I wanted her
narrow, long nose, her years on the kibbutz,
in the army, her goldsmith aunt in Haifa, the dread
that comes with being Israeli. I am only Jewish
by the relaxed standards of Reform or Nuremberg,
a mix of easter baskets and mezuzahs, but
in Israel, she said, we have amazing
beaches, and *everyone is beautiful and dark.*
I was brutal, and she loved it
in her tongue: *ken, ken, kaha, yes, ani gomeret,*
and I stole her skirt,
and I have never been to Israel.
I cannot pray.

MEGAN VOLPERT

I have two vampire hands

They are gypsy piano player slender with sharp scissor nails. People will say lesbians don't like this. What's good is the arch of a palm acquainted with throttle grips, the flurry of digits accustomed to occupying an imagination. My grandmother had these hands, gold chains cascading down both wrists while cursing. Couldn't read a lick of Hebrew, but was as superstitious as they come. Family tree branches into the chipper of world war while she dwelt on a girl who disappeared into the thicket. We are Transylvanian Jews and I did not tell my grandmother I was queer before she died, because I am quite sure she knew.

Mount Nebo

This is what happened in our other life:
we stared at the grit at the bottom of the cup,
a sorcerer's Rorschach that guaranteed felicity,
and we drank it, bitterness and all,
because in that other life –
the one in which we talked back to god,
convinced god to let us have both milk and honey in our cup
(the milk of our bodies, buttery kisses,
honeycomb caves perfected by stingerless bees) –
there is no pain, you see, no pain.
There is only fullness there.

I can see, I can see it from here.

SANDRA H. TARLIN

Secretly We Opened
the Bottle of Amber Sweetness
and Dipped Our Bread

Now the honey is hard, waxen, stored too long in a cold place.
My question spoken across the table, softens the hard place
where we are. "Do you want to make love?" "No!" you answer
      quickly,
"I have to go to the post office," and I see my grandmother rushing

toward the mailbox and away from the voice that has already told her
her sister has died in the Russian winter. We both fear
heavy trunks filled with quilts and mirrors.
What does it mean to be two lesbians, two Jews, speaking of
      separation?

I pace the apartment. I hear you enter the bedroom and shut the
      door.
When you open the door, I see you have placed a glass bowl
filled with fruit in the center of our bed; the sheets shine
against two plums and a cluster of green grapes.

I beg you to keep moving your fingers in and out of me.
I am naked and hot and strewn across the sheets,
but I feel as if I am a child under thick blankets,
 an edge of light making one eye open.

You are exhausted, you want to sleep.
How can I say I'm standing in steerage and don't know who I am?

HILARY LUSTICK

Wedding Vow

> *"We were not put on this earth to kill or to destroy*
> *We were put on this earth to praise, to labor, and to love."*
> —*Prayer for Peace*

I fear sinking into death once I get married, thinking
"married" is something you can ever really "get",
Thinking a person stops growing because she reaches "that point"
Thinking we can avoid the paths of our lives by hiding
in the rich shelter of another's undergrowth.
I won't make a vow for marriage.
I'll make a vow for peace.

I vow

To praise, separately, her,
Myself,
The Shechinah that lifted our eyes like Hadar,
Us, for grasping what it was we beheld.

I vow

To labor
for a home, a family, and a country
where more people can and want
to make vows like this one.

I vow

To love myself and my life,
to each day bring her a light, and not a void to be filled.
To love her when it's easy and when it is hard,
For her beauty and for all of her mystery.
I vow to love her as if I were her partner, with passion,
and to love her as if we were children, with total trust.
I vow to love her, whenever possible, as if we were nothing but
          souls,
with abandon, with no regard
for yesterday or tomorrow.
I vow to love like a spiraling wind.

I vow to praise, to labor, and to love
to keep this peace alive, and I write this
in prayer
for the humble strength to keep
my vows.

MARLA BRETTSCHNEIDER

An Ode to the Name
I Do Not Have

I might have changed my name
But I already have a Jewish tranny friend named Max
I love that name: Max
        It rocks.
So old world
        like Sadie and Heschie
Nostalgia- for an imagined Ashkenaz past

Max wasn't even my first choice
        as much as I'm drawn to it
I first explored Marx
Really

I'm named after my paternal grandfather, Marx
        my father's father
That's a bit too much masculinity
        even for my trans/formative genealogy
Though I'm attracted to the narrative of it

I'm named after a man named Marx
What a grand thing to be able to say

As a fellow traveler radical Jew, to serendipitously share the name

of this revolutionary produce of a long line of rabbis is a
democratically ennobling association.
The problem is,
with my anglo lingual flow,
it's just too hard to say

If I were to choose a new name as part of my genderfuck
I'd want it to be pleasing to the tongue
I'd need it to perform more oral satisfaction

Marx just feels too clumsy as a first name
My mouth fumbles in the dark
It interrupts the mojo

As a last name, Marx is great
Even in the boy language of using people's last names for address:
"Yo, Marx, over here"
I can hear my butch lover calling to me
I pull her close by the buckle on her jeans
I do love my girl boychick
But my genderqueer is not boyish. No one's home.

My friend Max is a generous spirit
a Talmud scholar
Not necessarily the: "I stick my flag in, therefore it's mine" type
ze might not care, I've never asked
she could say it would be fun to share
And so what, anyway, you say-
there are plenty of Maxs, Sophies and Abes

Still, we don't do our becoming in a vacuum
It feels overdone

Consider this an ode to the name I do not have
To the name I might have had
But it made no sense in "Ameerika"
And for a girl, feh
        Feh, what a gay word
                Ooh. Arouses desire perhaps to stir this pot anew

Meal Before the Fast

I'm sitting at the restaurant of my life
scouring the menu to decide my order and
the waitress arrives and I'm not ready yet indecision thrives
know what I should order but I don't
she goes away gives me time
then returns I explain
I was thinking of ordering the reality check special
but you know what…
I really don't want it
I want the entrée of denial instead sautéed with tunnel vision,
that comes with it right?
No she says, actually the tunnel vision is extra because of the
fastidiousness it takes the chef to ensure that it's secured atop
the entrée stays fixated and still doesn't roll over the sides
accessing its peripheral vision shift from tunnel to ocean view.

I want to go into Yom Kippur with a solid from the core answer of
how she feels about me and the thing is, I already know.
But I've been ignoring it cause the answer I think I need only
comes in a certain form and until I receive it in the perfect package
I can hold onto tunnel vision and wishful thinking
What can I do to get her to love me again?
let me count the ways ignore my own needs focus on hers
be what I think she wants me to be instead of accepting that

she is not who I want her to be

My Orthodox sister reminds me we go into Yom Kippur
not knowing our fate and
on Yom Kippur our fate is sealed.
I am forced to go into Yom Kippur yearning for her to love
me and knowing that she
did not call me back.

On my meal before the fast I'm going to change my order
Stop scarfing down denial cramming in every morsel panicked to
fill avoid hunger
I've been eating too fast forcing what I want down my throat
triggering my reflex esophagitis and it burns won't come up
go down can't breath
Instead I will
s l o w l y   c h e w   o n   r e a l i t y
see what it feels like on my teeth
Look down and
see what's really
on
my
plate.

DINAH KOMPANIETZA

Yom Kippur

I opened my eyes
old yachnas clustered around
with handbags
"will you break your fast?" they asked
and offered chocolate
I refused
not from piety but
because I felt perfectly all right
and embarrassed

standing in the balcony
the sound from downstairs
rose up in a muffled undulating stream
through the stuffy morning
it meandered on and on
while the colours
in the stained glass windows
gleamed in the sunlight and
the rich blue of the chairs
vibrated next to the blond wood of the rails

I looked out over women's hats
with bobbing feathers
and scanned the opposite balcony
until I found you
and thought
these long hours might be filled if I could inspect
the curve of your neck
as you leaned towards your mother and
tucked curly hair behind your ear
but then you looked up
and met my eyes
I fainted

ELEANOR LEVINE

Orgasm on Yom Kippur

humming through
the water faucet
I take breaths of
Lauren Hutton

legs find
radiation
from the metallic
idol
who thrusts me
to celestial
spheres of water sports

near shower
curtains
my mother
hovers above this
sacrilege
in
polyester
vestments

"pharmaceutical majors,
PhD scholars, and

lawyers," she declares,
"will get increasingly
sharp pains
in their vertebrae
if they illicitly
find pleasure in
the bathtub"

I break a disc
like a pebble falling
in the midst of
God's sacred words

ALLISON WONDERLAND

Everything I Need to Know about Being Jewish I Learned from The Nanny

Every *meshugeneh* needs a *mensch*
Don't *schlep* – get married already!
If you're over 30 and single
you might be–
–it's likely–
you're gay
(Oy vey!)
There'll be *kvetching* and *kibitzing*
You'll become a Jewcy bit of gossip
People will say *pish,* you're just *farmisht*
Your *mishpochah* will *plotz*
Start packing for your guilt trip
(Guilt: Just Jew it)

But what if you can't forget
about that little matzo ball of fire
you met at the synagogue
The one with charm and *chutzpah*
who makes your eyes light up like a menorah
your head spin like a dreidel
and your heart chant *Hava Nagila*
every time you look at her

What if you can't stop thinking
about the *meydl*
with the *sheyn ponem*
skin the color of honey
hair that flows like milk
and a body that wraps around yours
like the scrolls of the Torah

Don't let those *schmendricks*
rain on your parade
or make you feel *farchadat*
farfalen
or *farklempt*
Trade that guilt for (chocolate) *gelt*
break out the bubbly grape juice
and propose a toast —
to life
to love
to loving your life
and the woman in it

Your woman
Your love
Your chosen one

JULIE R. ENSZER

Testing Abraham

Perhaps he fancied himself Abraham,
the father of nations, but found himself
the father of three daughters, one now
long dead, the other two with no plans
to propagate—I wonder if we are
a cruel disappointment until I learn,
had my Dad been born ten or twenty years later,
reached maturity, post-Stonewall,
he might have found
himself without family or at least
not with our family, my mother,
my sisters, and me. His family
might have been like my adult family,
which wouldn't have existed because
I wouldn't be though that isn't the point,
this is: when I was running
the gay and lesbian community center
there was one group I didn't understand:
the bi married men.
They met once a month,
there were literally hundreds of them
and for the longest time
they were the only group to meet
on Saturday night. While

everyone else went to bars or concerts
or out on dates,
they gathered in secret, albeit
at the gay and lesbian center
where they would never tell us
their last names or even
a telephone number to contact the leader—
they always said they would call us to check in,
resolve problems, which they did,
regularly, quietly; still I didn't understand,
they had over three hundred and fifty men—
who were these men? why did they stay married?
were they really bisexual?
or just waiting to be gay?
what did their wives think?
did they have children?
so many questions and no answers,
not even after my sister
sneaked a peek at my father's email
on Christmas Eve and found,
well, I don't know what
exactly she found—I never asked—
she just called me crying
and accusatory *did I know?*
did I know my father was gay
or bi or whatever you call it when a man has a wife
and an apparent erotic interest in other men?
did I know? did I know?
I told her, *no, I didn't know,* which I didn't,

and I told her I was angry
that she read our father's email,
which I was, and that begat
a familial schism of Biblical proportions
in which I am just a scribe
who will bury this book and deny,
deny, deny all knowledge –
I'll pretend I'm Rebecca, daughter
of Bethuel, son of Nachor,
whom Milcah bore to him,
a stranger in a strange land
until I am drawn
into this family drama again.

MARGARITA MINIOVICH

on passover alone

this april it has snowed for three days
the trees barely recovered from winter
now stand defeated
their arms in white straight jackets
they thought they'd finally got away
they were wrong

i thought this crazy april would be a new beginning
i thought this crazy
i was wrong

this april i am alone
which is not new
i have almost gotten used to
a yellow balloon grown inside my chest long ago
in it lives a gnome
with neither history nor roots
without language or songs

i hate yellow
the balloon pushes against my ribs
makes it hard to breathe
i cannot find a needle to burst it
(where are sharp things when you need them?)
but then again, it would have to go straight through the heart

this crazy april i am alone on passover
tonight is the second seder
tonight is the second seder i sit
at my white ikea kitchen table
with my black half-persian cat on my lap
she is thrilled i am spending so much time at home

this crazy april i remember
not knowing about passover at all
for thirteen years of my life
(the yellow balloon sways left to right)

i remember learning to read my first hebrew words
the strange hieroglyphics becoming meaning
somewhere in the forgotten nucleus of my being
(the yellow balloon sways right to left)

i am surprised at the amount of room in my chest
my cage
for all this movement

i was thirteen
a refugee
freshly rootless

in the tiny two room school
in the tiny seaside town in italy
the russian immigrant kids
looked in the faces of eighty year old teachers

themselves from russia or poland long ago
now in italy to teach
the unfortunate
the ignorant
the stunned
the homesick
the shamed
the curious
russian jewish immigrant kids about being jewish

i looked at my eighty year old teachers
with brown liver spots
and blue decipherable numbers on their arms
their eyes burning with hope
and i learned to read and write hebrew
to sing songs
to build a succah
to say the word jew without whispering
or sweating in shame
or dying to be invisible
when my grandmother counted aloud the dead jews,
relatives buried alive in odessa

i learned about sweet oranges in haifa
white walls in jerusalem
the words six million
the word aliah
i learned about being wanted somewhere
and i wanted to go there

we came here instead
where i am "russian"
invisible, benign

this crazy april I am alone on passover
things i learned about being jewish -
a necklace of cool fresh water pearls and warm malachite
around the yellow balloon

but yellow obliterates all other shades
and I cannot remember anything but
the word haggadah and something about hard boiled eggs

the gnome grins, grunts
the thin string of pearls and malachite tumble down
and lodge themselves firmly in my gut

they are eyes now
watching me
watching me
i disappoint them
i am alone on passover
liquor stores are closed
i cannot even buy manishewitz

i close their stubborn eyelids
a dead face
nothing to look at

the snow keeps falling
on this endless night of the second seder

MAYA KUPERMAN *(Translation by Ran Shevi and Rotem Tashach)*

Selections from *Mother Tongue*

13

You love me like one loves a child:
With anger, with compassion, with need.
I love you like one loves a mother:
with hatred, fear, with wishes.
With shut eyes.
With the decisive notion that I, was brought substance into nothing -
and that I have to carry the is and the isn't together.
Nameless twins of a decisive fate

19

It happens that your eyes glisten in the dark.
Well versed in the language of forests,
picking cherries with your lips
and they answer you, giving themselves to your tongue.
Like them, naked on the cutting board
I have waited for you for years to perform a parting on me
in the glare of the knife of your gaze.

32

Your image rolls around in my lovers again and again.
I wake up at nights and see your face staring at me cold and asleep.
I blink, you disappear and my beloved returns.
I will forever carry your gaze, which grows distant, on my back
You will forever carry me within your amputated womb

BATYA WEINBAUM

Aleph (again)

And I walked down the streets with Sabrita. She had risen from the ocean playing her guitar, long curly disorganized locks, singing. She was the Sabra, Sabrita. So thin, curly hair, pile-lined boots in the winter when she was not barefoot in bed, and loose imitation leopard skin jacket at the towering top end of skin tight tye-dye pants. This was the first day I had walked back through the neighborhood after a night with her, again shopping for the nightgown. She wouldn't go in the girdle shop. We looked strange. We were outsiders. By myself I thought I could pass, but her contempt drizzled out of her as if she thought the neighborhood looked *galut,* like Jews in Diaspora.

MARILYN HACKER

For Despina

Why is it I don't like closing the curtains?
Even pinning pans of blue voile together
cuts me off too much from the winter morning's
comings and goings

and the tall, reassuring neighbors' windows
some with window boxes, some with their shades down
some cracked open from last night, so cold air could
refresh a sleeper.

Pick the stitch up, there in the place I dropped it.
Weave the ravelled sides of the day together
if December sun in a bedroom window
calls for a garment.

There are alphabets I could still decipher,
learn to read a stanza, or write my name in.
There are conjugations of verbs instructing
speech, song and silence.

Fear or hope or both of them made of me a
child who thought I'd probably be abandoned
if I misbehaved, if I lied about my
parents – or didn't.

How are you a Jew? asked the young Greek woman
First, because I haven't the choice to not be.
Those who thought they chose found the same unchosen
barbed wire and ashes.

How am I a Jew? Through my mother's birthright,
turned into a death-warrant once; excuse to
seize the farms and villages of a people
"exiled by exiles."

You, the dead, my interlocutors, whether
friends or strangers – child on a no-man's land, her
satchel and school uniform clear in gunsights,
riddled with bullets –

while I clutch the moment, with a safe childhood
as my history, no grandparents' village,
no street where her father made shoes, his mother
measured out barley.

Strange that all I know of them is – religion?
Not if they had land, sent their sons to cheder;
Not which ones spoke Yiddish, Hungarian, or
Polish, or German.

Not which child, renamed, fed the pigs and dug up
frozen mud for potatoes; not whose notebook
browned inside a cupboard, while trains moaned through the
Galician winter.

Must a murdered child, after generations,
be avenged by gunning down other children
far away from winter and pigs, potatoes
and nameless railroads?

"Preening left-wing Jews" mourn beside the cinder-
block debris where somebody's mother rolled up
cheese in dough while somebody's child unwisely
said, "Liberation."

If a Jew may not deconstruct the question
(two Jews, didn't we say, and three opinions?)
if they call the peacemakers anti-Semites,
who are my cousins?

Lost lands which I never would call my country…
How are you American ? she might ask me.
Language, economic determination…
Once, it was lucky.

ABOUT THE AUTHORS

JOAN ANNSFIRE's work has appeared in *The Harrington Lesbian Literary Quarterly, Sinister Wisdom, The SoMa Literary Review, 13th Moon, Bridges,* and *The Evergreen Chronicles.* Originally from Cleveland, OH, she now lives in Berkeley, CA.

ELLEN BASS's poetry books include *The Human Line,* named a Notable Book of 2007 by the San Francisco Chronicle, and *Mules of Love,* which won the Lambda Literary Award. Her poems have been published in *The Atlantic, The Kenyon Review, American Poetry Review* and many other journals. Her non-fiction books include *The Courage to Heal* and *Free Your Mind.* She teaches in the MFA program at Pacific University.

ROBIN BECKER's six collections of poems include *Domain of Perfect Affection, The Horse Fair, All-American Girl,* and *Giacometti's Dog.* Professor of English at The Pennsylvania State University, she has received individual fellowships for her poetry from The Bunting Institute, The Massachusetts Cultural Council, and the National Endowment for the Arts.

DR. MARLA BRETTSCHNEIDER is Professor of Political Philosophy with a joint appointment in Political Science and Women's Studies at the University of New Hampshire. She is founder and past Coordinator of Queer Studies there and currently serves as Coordinator of Women's Studies. Her most recent book is *The Family Flamboyant: Race Politics, Queer Families, Jewish Lives,* which won an IPPY Award.

LISA DORDAL holds a Master of Divinity and an MFA, both from Vanderbilt. Her poetry has appeared in the *Journal of Feminist Studies in Religion, Bridges: A Jewish Feminist Journal, Poems & Plays, Georgetown Review, Southern Women's Review* and *Cave Wall.* She lives in Nashville with her partner, Laurie, and their two retired greyhounds.

ELANA DYKEWOMON has been a cultural worker and activist since the 1970s. Her seven books include *Risk* (a 2010 Lambda nominee) and the award-winning historical novel, *Beyond the Pale*. Dykewomon was an editor of Sinister Wisdom for nine years; co-coordinated disabled and senior access for the SF Dyke March; offers private creative writing classes and editing – *www.dykewomon.org*. She lives in Oakland with her partner, Susan, stirring up trouble whenever she can.

JULIE R. ENSZER's first collection of poetry is *Handmade Love*. She also has published a chapbook, *Sisterhood*. She has an MFA from the University of Maryland and is enrolled currently in the PhD program in Women's Studies at Maryland.

JENNY FACTOR is the author of *Unraveling at the Name,* which won a Hayden Carruth Award and was a finalist for the Lambda Literary Award. She is a Core Faculty member in Poetry at Antioch University Los Angeles. She received her M.F.A. in Literature from the Bennington College Writing Seminars.

ROSE FOX's fiction and nonfiction have appeared in *Publishers Weekly, Strange Horizons,* the *Internet Review of Science Fiction,* and the anthology *Alleys & Doorways: Stories of Queer Urban Fantasy.* She lives in New York with one partner, two cats, five computers, and several thousand books.

MARILYN HACKER is a poet, critic, and reviewer. Her books of poetry include *Names; Going Back to the River; Love, Death, and the Changing of the Seasons;* and *Presentation Piece,* which won the National Book Award. Hacker won the PEN Award for Poetry in Translation for *King of a Hundred Horsemen* by Marie Étienne, which also earned the first Robert Fagles Translation Prize from the National Poetry Series. In 2010, she received the PEN/Voelcker Award for Poetry.

SHARRON HASS, poet and essayist, was born in Israel. She holds a B.A. in Classics and an M.A. in Religious Studies from Tel Aviv University. She published two volumes of poems, and participated in several international poetry festivals. Among her awards: The Hezy Leskly Award, the Ministry of Education and Culture Award, and the Prime Minister Award. She teaches literature and philosophy and lives in Tel Aviv.

JOANNA HOFFMAN is a spoken word poet originally from Silver Spring, Maryland. In 2007, she was the DC/Baltimore Grand Slam Champion and represented Baltimore at the Individual World Poetry Slam. She now performs with the Spoken Word Almanac Project. She is a graduate of the NYU Wagner Graduate School of Public Service, and works at a nonprofit organization.

ERYCA KASSE is a 37 year old, white, Jewish lesbian writer and poet of the written and spoken word. She is a social worker with adults in mental health and addictions recovery, and incorporates writing therapy into the group and individual therapeutic process. She lives in DC with her two cats Nina and Olive.

MELANIE KAYE/KANTROWITZ is a writer and poet, activist, scholar and teacher. A pioneer in women's studies, she taught the first such course at the University of California at Berkeley in Comparative Literature, where she earned her Ph.D. She lives with her lover and their dog in Queens.

BONNILEE KAUFMAN is a Learning Disabilities Specialist for the California Community Colleges and a workshop presenter for GLIDE (Gays & Lesbians Initiating a Dialogue for Equality). Her work has previously been published in the anthology *Ghosts of the Holocaust*.

DINAH KOMPANIETZA writes on a variety of subjects, in different genres. She writes poetry in the name of her great-grandmother. She will always be indebted to Berta Freistadt z"l, her first editor.

MAYA KUPERMAN is an award-winning Israeli poet and a journalist and one of the central lesbian voices active in the country today. Born and raised in Haifa, Kuperman started publishing in literary magazines at the age of 16. Her book of poems *Mother Tongue* was published in 2007. She studied Comparative Literature and Gender Studies in Tel-Aviv University and recently moved to Berlin to begin her MA studies in English Literature.

ELEANOR LERMAN is the author of the novel *Janet Planet*, two short story collections and five books of poetry, most recently *The Sensual World Re-emerges*. She has received fellowships from the National Endowment for the Arts and the Guggenheim Foundation, and has won the Lenore Marshall Prize, among many other honors and nominations.

ELEANOR LEVINE's work has been published in *The Washington Blade*, *The New York Blade*, *The New York Native*, *The Denver Quarterly*, *Fiction*, *The California Quarterly*, *The Toronto Quarterly Magazine* and other publications. She holds an MFA in Creative Writing from Hollins University. She is currently a medical copy editor in New Jersey and lives in Philadelphia with her dog, Virginia Woolf.

JOY LADIN, David and Ruth Gottesman Professor of English at Stern College of Yeshiva University, has published five books of poetry: *Coming to Life*, *Psalms*, *Transmigration*, *The Book of Anna* and *Alternatives to History*. She is also the author of a forthcoming collection of autobiographical essays on gender transition, *Who Will Be: A Woman Caught in the Act of Becoming*, and a critical study, *Soldering the Abyss: Emily Dickinson and Modern American Poetry*.

HILARY LUSTICK's work has previously been published in *13th Moon* and *On the Fence*. She received an Honorable Mention from the American Poets Prize in 2003. She teaches 10th grade English in Brooklyn, New York, where she is also involved in education organizing.

JENNIFER MARGULIES is a poet, playwright, and the co-founder and editor of Evelyn Street Press. Her poetry has been published in *Borderlands: Texas Poetry Review*. Her poem "Timepiece" was selected for the Blanton Museum of Art's ekphrastic poetry project. She currently lives in Syracuse, New York with her partner and their baby daughter.

MARGARITA MINIOVICH is a Jewish lesbian writer and poet. She immigrated to Canada from Russia at the age of 13. Her work has been published in two issues of *Fireweed* and in the anthology *Friday the Rabbi Wore Lace*. She is the 2010 first prize winner of the First Person

Narrative National Essay Contest run by the Canadian Lesbian and Gay Archives and her essay will be published in the *Keeping Our Stories Alive* anthology.

BONNIE J. MORRIS is a women's history professor at both George Washington University and Georgetown, the author of eight books, including three Lambda Literary Award finalists: *Eden Built By Eves, Girl Reel,* and *Revenge of the Women's Studies Professor.*

JOAN NESTLE is a white, Jewish, working class fem lesbian from the Bronx who now lives in Brunswick, Australia. Nestle is an author, historian, and co-founder of the Lesbian Herstory Archives in New York City.

LESLÉA NEWMAN is the author of the poetry collections, *Still Life with Buddy, Nobody's Mother, Signs of Love,* and the forthcoming *October Mourning: A Song for Matthew Shepard.* She is a recipient of a poetry fellowship from the National Endowment for the Arts, and a past poet laureate of Northampton, Massachusetts. She teaches at Spalding University's brief residency MFA in Writing program.

JESS NOVAK is from New York City and rural Virginia. She is a queer activist and currently pursuing a MFA in poetry at Florida State University. Her work appears in *In Posse Review.*

ACHY OBEJAS is the author of the novels Ruins, *Days of Awe,* and *Memory Mambo,* the short story collection *We Came All the Way From Cuba So You Could Dress Like This?,* and the poetry collection *This Is What Happened In Our Other Life.* She is also the editor and translator of *Havana Noir,* and has received an NEA Fellowship in Poetry. *www. achyobjeas.com*

ELLEN ORLEANS is the author of the play *"God, Guilt, and Gefilte Fish: An Unorthodox Comedy"* and five books of queer humor and commentary, including *Can't Keep A Straight Face* and *The Butches of Madison County.* Her short story, *"Comfort,"* about the invention of bagels, latkes, and matzo balls, appears in the anthology *Primal Picnics.*

Originally from New Jersey, she lives in Boulder, CO, where she runs the *Yellow Pine Reading Series*.

SIMA RABINOWITZ is the author of *The Jewish Fake Book* and *Murmuration*. Recent publications include poems and essays in *Sentence, Trivia, Hamilton Arts & Letters, South Loop Review*, and *Water-Stone Review*. She served as the first writer-in-residence at Yeshiva University Museum in New York and recently received a BRIO Award from the Bronx Council on the Arts.

SANDRA H. TARLIN is Associate Professor of English at Bronx Community College, CUNY. She received her Ph.D. in English and Creative Writing from the University of Houston. Her poems have appeared in journals such as *Ark/angel Review, Bridges, Mobius, Poetica, Sinister Wisdom* and *Western Humanities Review*. She has been the recipient of the PSCUNY grant, an Anna Davidson Rosenberg Award for Poems on the Jewish Experience, and the Inprint Barthelme Fellowship for Poetry.

MEGAN VOLPERT's fourth book is *Sonics in Warholia*. She is Co-Director of the Atlanta Queer Literary Festival, has an MFA from Louisiana State University, and works as a high school English teacher.

BATYA WEINBAUM, editor of *Femspec*, teaches at SUNY ESC CDL. She has published poetry in *Heresies, Key West Review, Feminist Review, Mountain Laurel, Reclaiming, Thoughfrime, Valley Advocate*, and *Catharsis*.

ALLISON WONDERLAND *(http://aisforallison.blogspot.com)* has a B.A. in Women's Studies. Her work appears in *Gertrude, Passionate Hearts, Best Lesbian Romance 2009, Coming Together: At Last, Visible: A Femmethology*, and *To Love and To Cherish*.

A MIDSUMMER NIGHT'S PRESS was founded by Lawrence Schimel in New Haven, CT in 1991. Using a letterpress, it published broadsides of poems by Nancy Willard, Joe Haldeman, and Jane Yolen, among others, in signed, limited editions of 126 copies, numbered 1-100 and lettered A-Z. One of the broadsides—"Will" by Jane Yolen—won a Rhysling Award. In 1993, the publisher moved to New York and the press went on hiatus until 2007, when it began publishing perfect-bound, commercially-printed books, primarily under two imprints:

FABULA RASA: devoted to works inspired by mythology, folklore, and fairy tales. The first titles from this imprint are Fairy Tales for Writers by Lawrence Schimel, *Fortune's Lover: A Book of Tarot Poems* by Rachel Pollack, *Fairy Tales in Electri-city* by Francesca Lia Block, and the forthcoming *The Last Selchie Child* by Jane Yolen.

BODY LANGUAGE: devoted to texts exploring questions of gender and sexual identity. The other titles from this imprint are *This is What Happened in Our Other Life,* the first collection of poems from Lambda Literary Award-winner Achy Obejas; *Banalities* by Brane Mozetic, translated from the Slovene by Elizabeta Zargi with Timothy Liu; *Handmade Love* by Julie R. Esnzer; and *Mute* by Raymond Luczak.